Sound and Music

Mountain Word Academy

from the Mount St Helens Creation Center

Physics

Paul F Taylor, BSc MEd

Physics: Sound and Light

Published by:

J6D Publications

PO Box 629

Castle Rock, WA 98611

USA

www.justsixdays.com

www.mshcreationcenter.org

mwacademy.mshcreationcenter.org

Copyright © 2019 by Paul F Taylor

The right of Paul F Taylor to be identified as author of this work has been asserted by him in accordance with the Copyright, Designs, and Patents Acts 1988, and by all international copyright agreements.

Scripture quotations are from the ESV® Bible (The Holy Bible, English Standard Version®), copyright © 2001 by Crossway, a publishing ministry of Good News Publishers. Used by permission. All rights reserved.

Where possible, copyright permissions have been noted for all illustrations used. Photographs taken by the author can be assumed to be licensed as Creative Commons Share-Alike Attribution 4.0 International. All images are reproduced by permission.

ISBN: 978-1-7337363-0-5

J6D Publications is an official publications imprint, through Kindle Direct Publishing - a division of Amazon; kdp.amazon.com

Contents

1. Music in the Bible

The story of music in the Bible is a vast subject. People have written whole books on the subject, and we are going to attempt to say something in just two pages! Clearly, there is a lot more study to be done on this subject, and there are many other books that you should read, to get to grips with what the Bible actually says about music.

However, this is a scientific textbook. That does not mean that we will ignore the artistic merits of music, nor how it reflects God's creativity. But our primary focus is on the science or physics of sound and music.

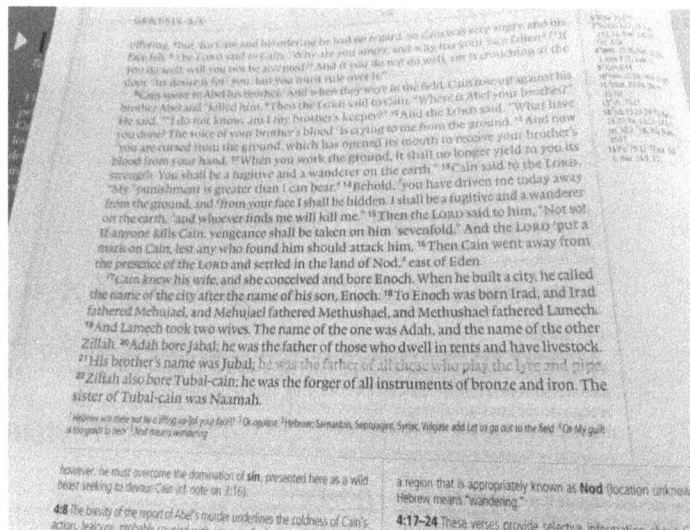

Genesis 4

Music is first mentioned in the Bible in Genesis 4. One of the son's of Cain's descendant, Lamech, was a man called Jubal. Jubal was described in verse 21 as "the father of all those who play the lyre and pipe". This fleeting mention is sufficient to tell us a few important things about music.

1. There are two types of melodic musical instruments mentioned. The first is the lyre, representing stringed instruments. A string or wire is set to vibrate, to produce the note.

2. Second, there are wind instruments, represented here by the pipe. A tube encloses air, which is set to vibrate in some way.

3. Since Jubal is a descendant of both Lamech and Cain - neither of whom were nice people, to put it mildly - it shows that music can be used for good or for ill. A great deal of the Bible describes the use of music in the worship of the Lord, but we also see that music can be used for purposes which are not good, and do not conform to God's will. Indeed, most types of music can be used for either good or ill.

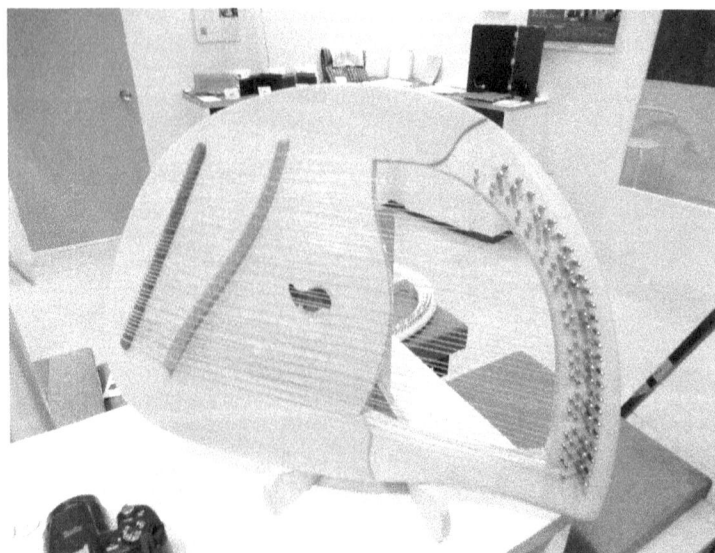

This "modern" twist on the lyre was made in 1926, but shows the clear use of a bridge, tuning pins, and even a soundbox.

Worship

We see music used principally in a positive context in the act of worship. The Psalms are, perhaps, the most obvious place where we see music mentioned. Indeed, the Psalms are actually songs or hymns. Many of them give details about the tune, to which they are to be sung, as well as

The Shofar is a wind instrument, played a bit like a trumpet, and made from a ram's horn.

comments about the musical instruments to be used. There are suggestions by some that the frequent use of the word *selah* denotes the incorporation of an instrumental section, before singing restarts.

Harps and Lyres

A biblical harp would have been played similarly to a modern harp - or maybe with a bow. It was a weighty instrument, a about three feet in height. At its base was a bulbous sound chamber, and two large animal horns were inserted into this. Five strings were placed on one side, and another five on the other. These were fixed, so that once they had been tuned, it would not be possible to adjust them. It is thought likely that the ten strings were tuned to:

$$E2 - F2 - F\#2 - G2 - G\#2 - A2 - A\#2 - B2 - C3 - D3$$

where C4 is middle c.

Lyres would have had tunable strings. Some early lyres may not have had a soundbox, though modern reconstructions of them usually do. It is also the case that the terms harp and lyre are often interchangeable, due to their common descent.

Shofar and Pipes

The pipes are the ancestors of modern woodwind instruments, which are now made of wood or metal. They would probably have had a reed - possibly even a double reed, like an oboe. Biblical pipes would usually have been made of wood, though metal pipes are also possible.

The shofar is the ancestor of the modern trumpet, and would have had to be played by the musician adopting an *embouchure*. However, the instrument was made out of horn - which is why modern brass instruments are often called horns. The horn of a ram would have been hollowed out to make the instrument, and it would have relied entirely on harmonics to make the notes.

For Further Study

Take some time to find a passage in the Bible that refers to the use of music. Write some notes and comments about the way the passage is discussing the use of music.

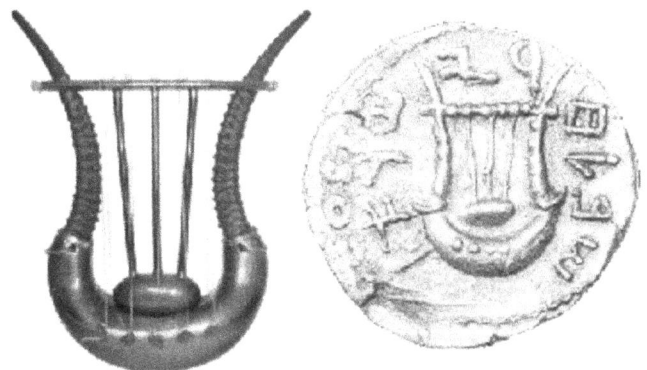

From musicofthebible.com

2. Science and Music

One of the main reasons why music is useful to us, in our scientific study of sound, is that it gives us a number of terms, and their definitions, which are helpful to us in our scientific study of sound.

Harmonic Motion

Harmonic motion is a cyclical type of motion. It can be seen in the motion of a balance wheel, or a pendulum. As we will see, it also describes how various types of energy can be transferred by waves. The simplest type of harmonic motion is called, understandably, *simple harmonic motion* (SHM). The mathematical formulae for a body undergoing simple harmonic motion shows that the acceleration of the body is constantly changing, and works in the direction opposite to that of the motion. In SHM, the acceleration is actually proportional to the displacement of an object, from its center of oscillation. An object moving away from the center of oscillation will, therefore, eventually slow down, and be moved back to the center, overshooting it, and then being slowed from that direction. Such motion can therefore be described by this formula:

$$a = -c^2x$$

a represents acceleration; x is the displacement from the center of oscillation; c is any real number, hence c^2 is a positive number.

Such harmonic motion can be seen in a number of simple oscillation objects. For example, a mass attached to a spring can be set oscillating by displacing the mass downwards slightly. The mass will bob up and down, and keep doing so, if it is not being damped. (In practice, of course, it is being damped, by air resistance, but this will be negligible for initial measurements). Another example is a pendulum, swinging back and forth.

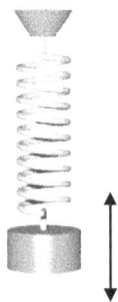

There is a relationship between simple harmonic motion and circular motion. Consider a point light on the outside of a circle, which is rotating in a plane 90° to your line of sight. Imagine that it is circuiting at a constant rate. Now imagine viewing the circle edge on. The light would appear to be going up and down, and would be doing so at a rate defined by simple harmonic motion.

Definitions

Now we need a few definitions. The **time period** (T) is the time that it takes for the oscillating object to get back to its starting point. So, with the mass on a spring, when it is released, it will travel upwards, and then downwards again. When it reaches its lowest point again, the time taken to do this is T. Another important measurement would be the number of oscillations per second. This value is the **frequency** (f). So frequency and time period are related by:

$$f = \frac{1}{T}$$

Sound

Sound oscillations can be measured by an oscilloscope. Although the old fashioned cathode ray oscilloscopes that laboratories used to have a expensive, there are some free apps that work on smartphones or tablets that work very well. I have been using one which is called SmartScope Oscilloscope, from LabNation. This app is really intended to be used with the LabNation's SmartScope interface, which looks like a very good piece of kit, but it can be used with the microphone input of your phone or tablet, including with an input into the microphone jack (which will probably need a splitter adapter). I use this on a 10 inch Lenovo tablet, running Android. It is free from Google Play. A sound input produces a wave. This can be frozen by tapping camera icon.

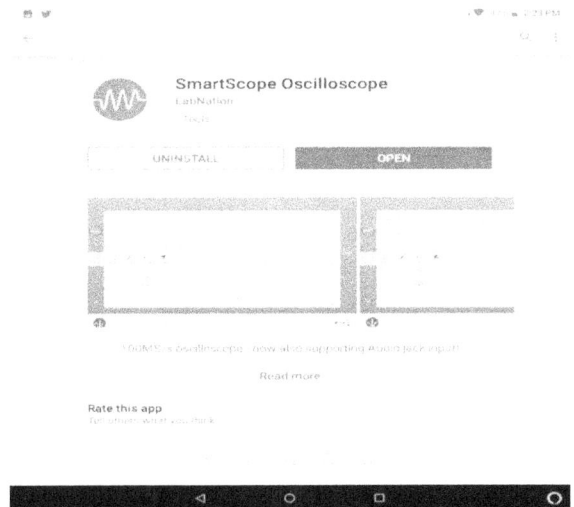

Oscilloscope app in Google Play

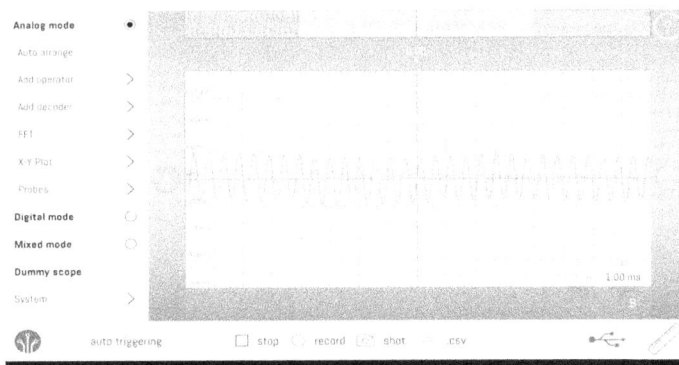

The graph produced on the oscilloscope is of displacement against time. The graph shown was obtained by the oscilloscope app, as I whistled into it.

Activity and Further Study

Get some different screenshots, showing the displacement / time plots for a number of different sounds. Try sounds of different loudness, different pitch, and, maybe, different musical instruments. If possible, compare the graph produced for a "real" instrument with the synthesized sound of that same instrument produced on an electronic keyboard. What are the differences produced by the different instruments? What do you understand by the units shown on the graphs? Look them up, and relate them to the qualities that you think are being produced by your sounds.

3. String Sounds

Now we are in a position to investigate some types of musical instruments, and see what information we can derive from them. To recap - there are basically two types of melody instruments, which are string and wind. Of course, there are percussion instruments, and some of these may be tuned (such as a xylophone) but we will treat these separately. We will also treat modern synthesized instruments separately as well.

Stringed instruments will include the following list, though I could well have omitted your favorite!

Violin family (violin, viola, cello, double bass), guitars, harps, lyres, piano, harpsichord etc.

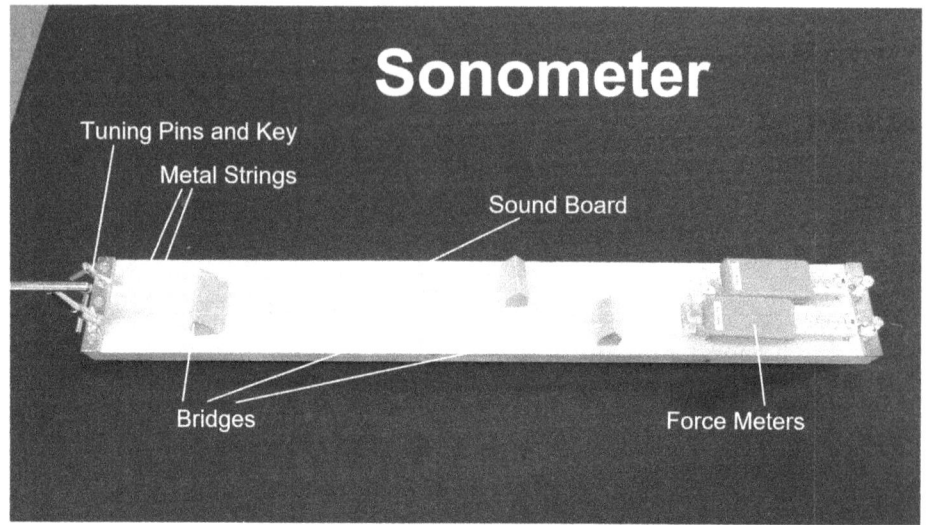

Sonometer

A useful scientific instrument to test the concept of a stringed instrument is a sonometer. This sonometer was purchased from Sci-Supply, through Amazon.

The sonometer is built and used as follows. A wooden base serves as a sound board. Two metal strings, of different cross-sectional areas (thicknesses) are stretched across. Wooden bridges can be moved, to select lengths of string to vibrate. At one end, the strings are attached with tuning pins, to apply force (tension) into the string. A key assists with the accurate turning of the tuning pins. At the other end, the strings are attached to force meters. Regrettably, these meters are erroneously measuring kilograms, which is a unit of mass not force. The should be measuring force in newtons (N). However, for the accuracy of these experiments, you can assume that 1kg represents 10N. You will need some other apparatus. You will need a meter rule, or a tape measure, to measure the lengths of the strings. We will be measuring lengths in millimeters or centimeters - not inches. To estimate the pitch of the notes produced, you could have an electronic keyboard nearby and / or a set of tuning forks.

Pitch vs Length

In this experiment, adjust the bridges so that the length of the string being vibrated is 40cm. Then adjust the tension, checking the pitch against a standard tuning fork. In the diagram, a C4 standard tuning fork is struck and placed on a sound box. The C4 fork vibrates at 256Hz (Hz stands for Hertz and is the number of oscillations per second). Measure the tension in newtons (in the above example, a tension of 24N was recorded.

Now, without changing the tension, move the smaller bridge closer to the larger bridge, until the pitch of the string matches a C5 tuning fork (512Hz). Record the length. What do you notice?

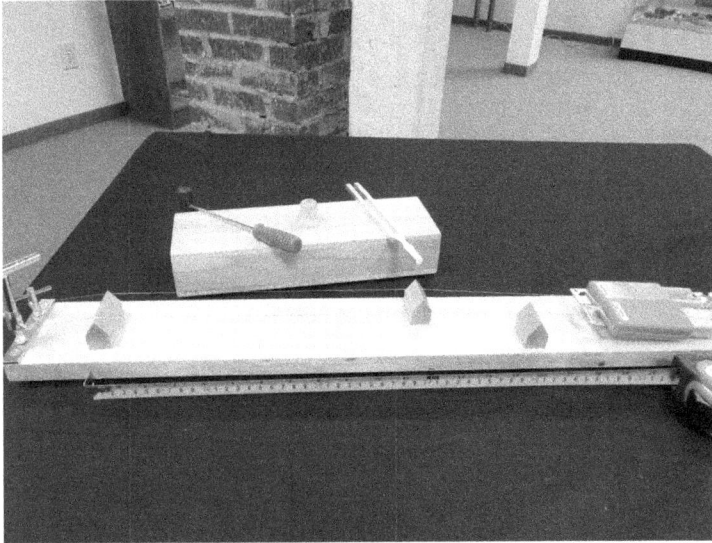

If your ears are good at hearing pitch, move the smaller bridge again, until you get the next C (C6, at 1024Hz). Record the length. What do you notice?

In the example shown, C4 had been set to 40cm. C5 was 20cm, and C6 was 10cm. Every octave requires half the previous length, provided no other factors have been changed.

Now find the lengths that match a range of tuning forks, or keyboard keys,; preferably a musical major scale from C4 through C5.

When these figures are plotted on a chart, and a smooth curve drawn through them, we see that we have a hyperbole. With fixed cross-sectional area and tension, the frequency is inversely proportional to the length of the string.

Standing Wave

Sound waves in musical instruments are usually represented as standing waves. This is where the wave forms oscillate in sync, so that there are points of no oscillation (nodes), and halfway between these are points of maximum oscillation (anti-nodes).

With a vibrating string, both ends of the strings are at minimum or no oscillation. This makes them nodes. Therefore, with a normal vibration, the wavelength (λ) of the sound wave will be twice the length of the string.

For Further Study

Set the string length back to 40cm. In another set of experiments, keep the length constant at 40cm, but change the tension in the string, to match the string to each of the tuning forms in turn. Plot a graph of frequency against tension, and derive a relationship between them.

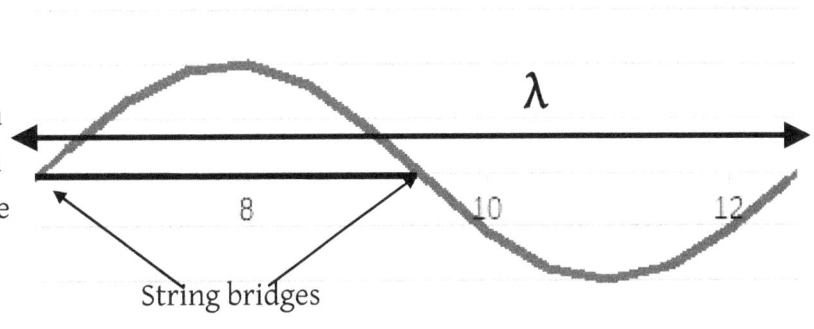

String bridges

One important relationship that you will note is as follows: Every octave doubles the frequency of vibration.

What is the numerical relationship between notes of a perfect 5th apart? - i.e. C4-G4, D4-A5 etc.

4. String Sounds continued

Recap

From the previous spread, we derive the following from your further study.

The relationship between frequency and tension appears to be linear. However, the line does not cut the axis at the origin. This is because the linear relationship breaks down at very low tensions.

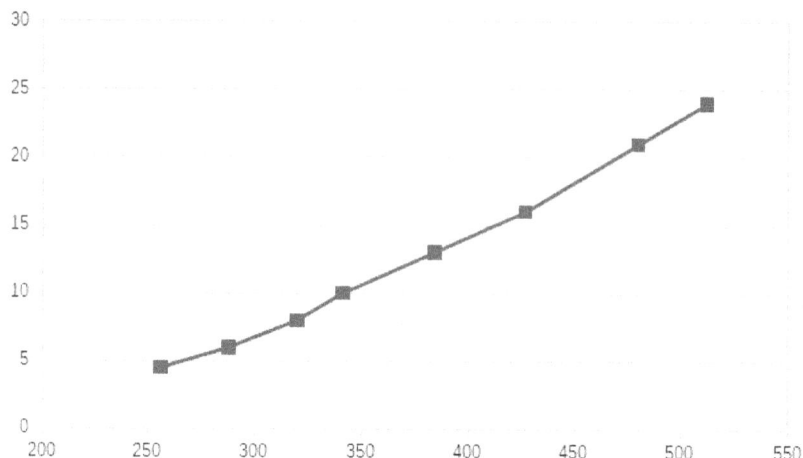

We also notice that if we divide the frequency of a note by the frequency of the note a perfect fifth below, we get the factor 1.5.

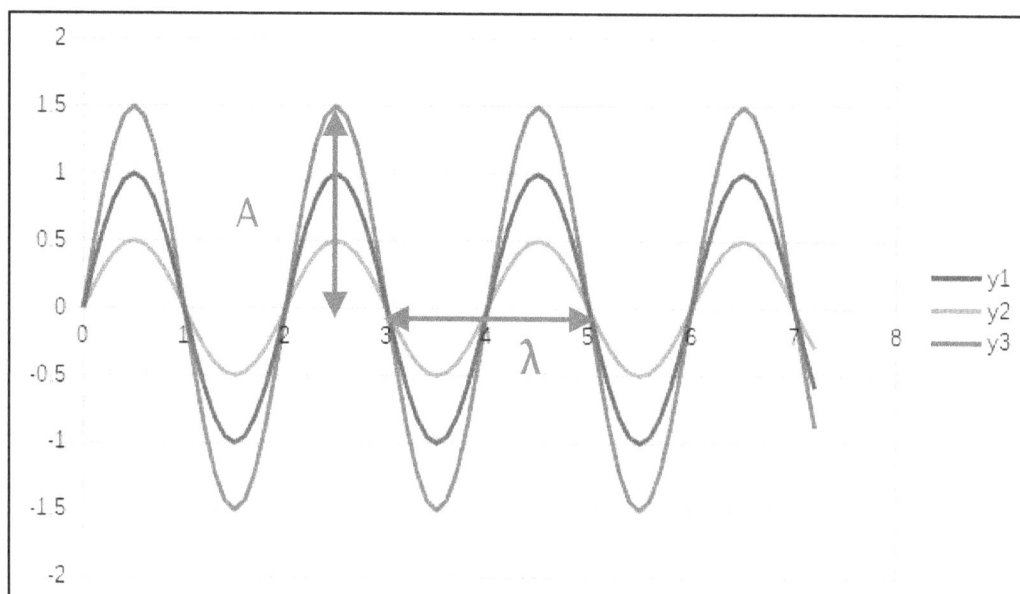

Definitions

In this diagram, three waves have been superimposed. They all have the same wavelength, so they all have the same pitch. However, the waves' anti-nodes are at different levels of energy. The distance from the origin to the top of a peak (crest) is the *amplitude* ('A) and is related to the loudness or volume of the sound.

Simple tests with the sonometer will show you that lower pitched notes have longer wavelengths and shorter frequencies. Higher pitched notes will have shorter wavelengths and higher frequencies.

The wavelength is the length of one cycle. The frequency is the number of cycles per second. If we multiply these values, we have the distance traveled per second, which is the speed (or, more correctly, the velocity) of the wave. So multiplying the wavelength by the frequency of a sound with give you the speed of sound.

Harmonics

Musical sounds are always complicated by *harmonics*. The study of harmonics is very interesting, both scientifically, and artistically. Players of stringed instruments, such as guitars, are often adept at producing harmonics.

Scientifically, a harmonic sequence relies on the fact that a string vibrates with a node at both bridges. But these do not have to be consecutive nodes.

Set your sonometer string at a length an tension to match C4. I suggest a fairly long length, so try 40cm, as before. Pluck the string as hard as you can. Then touch the string gently and rapidly at the 20cm mark (exactly halfway. What do you hear? You should hear note C5, faintly. This is the first harmonic. It occurs because the swift, gentle touch at the halfway point adds an extra node, halfway along the string, so you get a vibration of half the wavelength (therefore twice the frequency) of the natural, or root note.

The second harmonic is much harder to obtain. Again, pluck the string hard, and touch gently and rapidly at a point about 13.3 cm from one end (a third). This imposes two extra nodes, at 1/3 and 2/3 along the string. This makes a wavelength of 1/3 of the original, or a frequency of 3 times the original. The 2nd harmonic therefore has a frequency 1.5 times the 1st harmonic, and must be G5. The third harmonic is C6, and the fourth is E6. The fifth harmonic does not really fit with a Western music scale.

This diagram shows a sonometer string vibrating at natural frequency, and first and second harmonics.

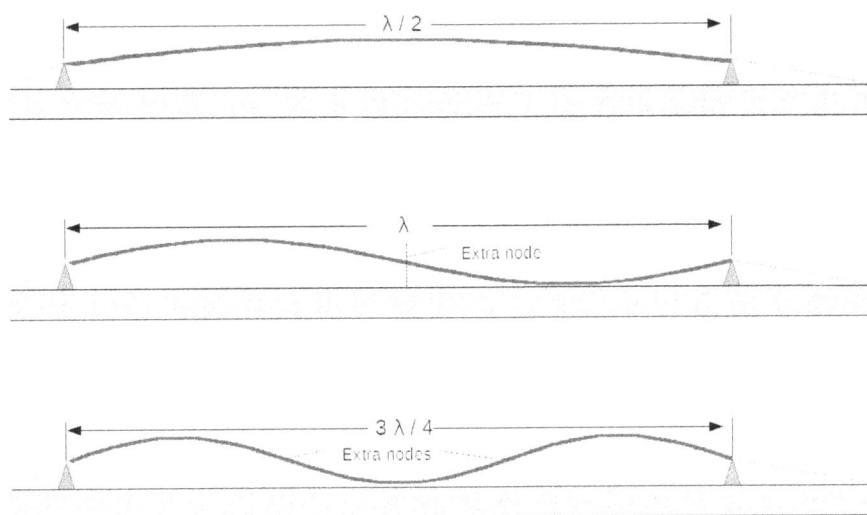

For Further Study

Find out some further uses of harmonics in stringed instruments.

5. Transverse and Longitudinal Waves

It is time that we looked at the different types of waves that exist. To do this, we will need to take a slight bunny trail, and look at examples of waves other than just sound.

So far, we have looked at graphs of waves, by plotting the displacement (movement away from and towards the origin) against the distance moved. The wave has a two-dimensional appearance on the chart.

Transverse Waves

There are a number of waves that look physically like the wave we have just described above. We can see am easy physical representation of such a wave, by using the children's toy known as a *slinky*. This is a coiled spring. In order to simulate a wave, attach one end to a fixed point, such as a hook placed on the wall at floor level. Then stretch the spring. Do not over stretch. Never stretch the slinky past the elastic limit - that is, the point beyond which it won't return to its original shape.

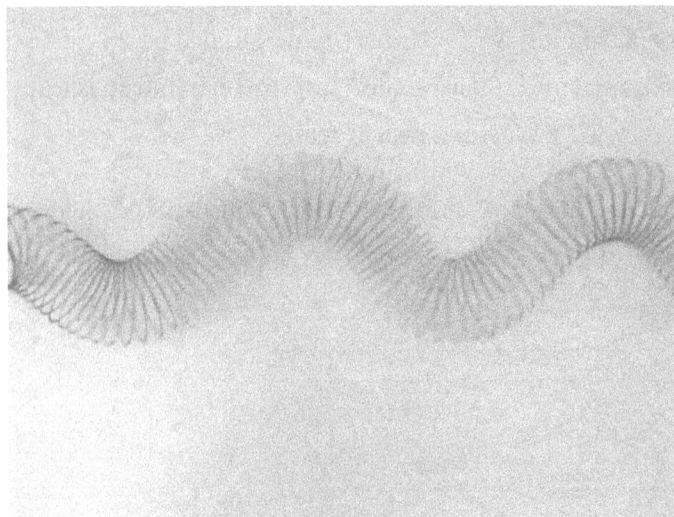

Now, keeping the slinky along the ground, rapidly move the end you are holding from side to side, at right-angles to the direction of the spring. This should cause a wave to move along the spring.

Light travels by transverse waves. Light is a somewhat unusual type of wave, in that the medium which is oscillating is not a material, but rather the electromagnetic field. Earthquake S-waves are also transverse waves, traveling through the body of the Earth from the earthquake source.

Longitudinal Waves

Sound waves do not travel as transverse waves. They travel as longitudinal waves. A longitudinal wave is one where the displacement is in the same direction (parallel) to the motion

Longitudinal waves

Longitudinal waves fluctuate in the same direction as the wave is travelling

Transverse waves

Transverse waves fluctuate at a right angle to the direction that the wave is travelling

theconversation.com   Creative Commons License

Compressional Wave

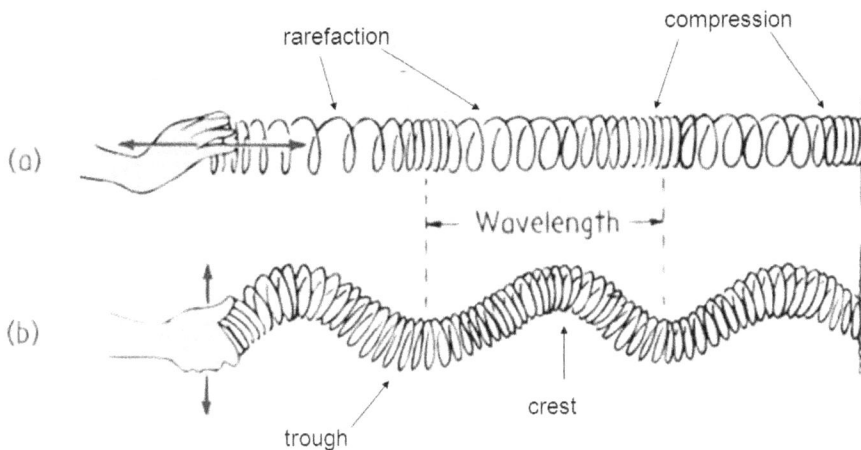

Transverse Wave

of the wave. What this looks like in practice is a series of compressions and rarefactions traveling. Longitudinal waves can be simulated with a slinky by rapidly moving the hand forward and backward.

When a sound is created, air molecules near the source are compressed. These then compress the next set of molecules, while the previous set expand in a rarefaction. By this method the compression of successive gas molecules transfers the energy through the air, until these compressions hit the eardrum, or *timpanic membrane*. The wavelength can be measured from the center of one compression to the next. Although these sort of waves appear to be straight lines, it still makes sense to draw a displacement / distance graph with the variables at right angles in the chart, even though we know they are actually in the same direction.

Other examples of longitudinal waves include earthquake P-waves.

When an earthquake happens, the source causes transfer causes energy to be transferred by two different wave forms - P and S waves. The faster of the two are P-waves. The S-waves arrive some 70% of the timescale later.

For Further Study
Discuss this sentence, taken from Salter-Horner Physics. Correct it and rewrite it.

When hands are clapped, air is squashed between them and exerts an opposing force, pushing the hands apart again. The to-and-fro movement creates a series of compressed and rarefied areas in the surrounding air so that air pressure is changed. The compression exits. The compressions are regions below atmospheric pressure and rarefactions are regions of higher pressure. The compressions and rarefactions travel outwards in the plane of the clapping hands as a sound wave. When the pressure changes reach the loudspeaker. They are immediately converted into electrical signals, generating a voltage which flows onto the oscilloscope and onto the screen. This makes the oscilloscopic trace appears to dump.

6. Wind Instrument Sounds

Put simply, a wind instrument is basically a tube, and the sound is caused by vibrating air. The actual mode of causing the air to vibrate differs greatly from instrument to instrument. But we can simplify our study of wind instrument sounds by simply assuming that such an instrument will behave like a tube. In some cases, the tube will be open at both ends. In others, the tube will be open at one end only.

Closed-end Tune

First, let's consider a tube which has one open end and one closed end. Suppose the length of the tube is L. The closed end will be a node and the open end will be an anti-node. The diagram below shows the relationship between L and the wavelength, λ.

$$\lambda = 4\,L$$

The situation is not quite as simple as this diagram makes it appear, however. It is also possible to get a node at one end, and an anti-node at the open end, by having multiple nodes and anti-nodes. Tubes of air will vibrate with a large number of harmonics, and the overall sound is actually a combination of the various harmonic waves included. Here are some of the other harmonics included.

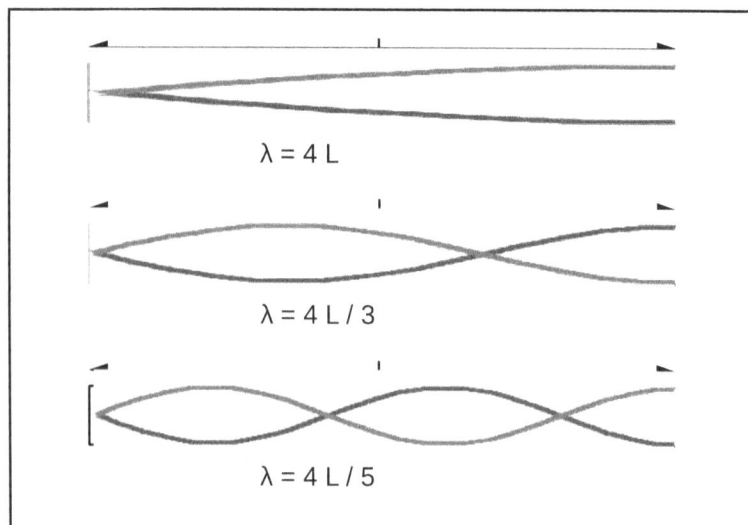

$\lambda = 4\,L$

$\lambda = 4\,L / 3$

$\lambda = 4\,L / 5$

Tube Open Both Ends

If the tube is open at both ends, then there will be an anti-node at both ends. Work out what you think the wave will look like for the natural note, in an open tube of length L, and sketch it. Also sketch the first two harmonics for this open tube, and find the relationship between L and λ for all three situations.

Resonance Tube Activity

This activity gives a very accurate relationship between wavelength and frequency, and enables us accurately to calculate the speed of sound. We need to have a tube, closed at one end, but where the closed end can be moved, so that the length L can be varied. This is achieved by closing the end of the tube with water, and having a water reservoir attached, by means of which the water level can easily be changed. The photograph shows such an arrangement.

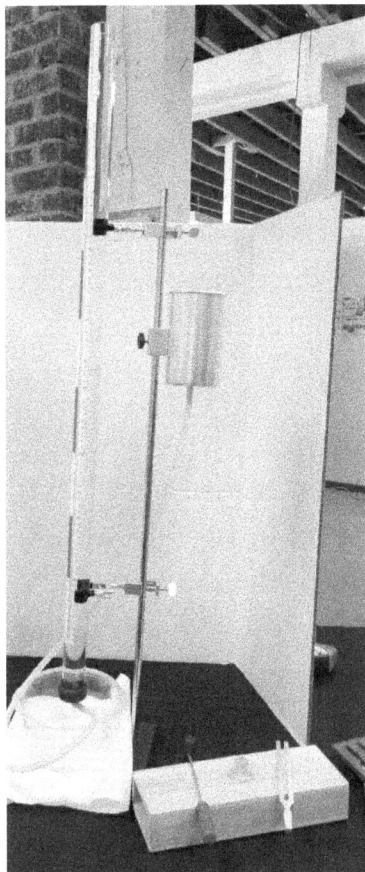

The aluminum container is a reservoir of water, attached to the bottom of the measuring tube by some flexible plastic tube. The reservoir can be slid up and down the stand. This causes the water level in the measuring tube to change. The height of the air column in the measuring (resonance) tube can be obtained from the scale attached to the tube's side; just measure the height from the top to the water level.

The experiment really needs two people (or one person with three hands!). A tuning fork is struck, and held over the top of the resonance tube, not quite touching the glass. The water level is adjusted, until a louder resonance of the tuning fork's note is heard. It may be necessary to re-strike the tuning fork periodically. When resonance is achieved, note the tube height. However, there is more than one resonance point, because of the harmonic situation described above. So there should be three, maybe four, height measurements for each tuning fork frequency. Working out whether a resonance height represents the natural, first, or second harmonic will involve a little bit of educated guesswork in the analysis of the numbers. Remember that the frequency on the tuning form represents the natural note, not any of the harmonics. When you have adjudged how the heights relate to harmonics, it should be possible to work out the wavelength of the natural note for each frequency. The speed of sound - v - will be found by the formula:

$$V = f * \lambda$$

To obtain one set of results, I used a C5 (512Hz) tuning fork. A quick run through the experiment provided resonance points at 0.15m, 0.45m, and 0.75m. These were assumed to correspond to $\lambda/4$, $3\lambda/4$, and $5\lambda/4$ respectively. As the 0.45m reading was in the middle of the range, I re-measured this, much more carefully and accurately, and got the result 0.448m. This yields a wavelength value of 0.597m.

So the speed of sound is found by the above formula.

$$V = 512 \times 0.597$$

$$\therefore v = 305.7 \text{ ms}^{-1}$$

This is fairly close to the literature value of 343 ms-1, though not as close as we would like.

For Further Study

How could the experiment be improved, to give a more reliable value? If you have several tuning forks, how can they be utilized to give more accuracy?

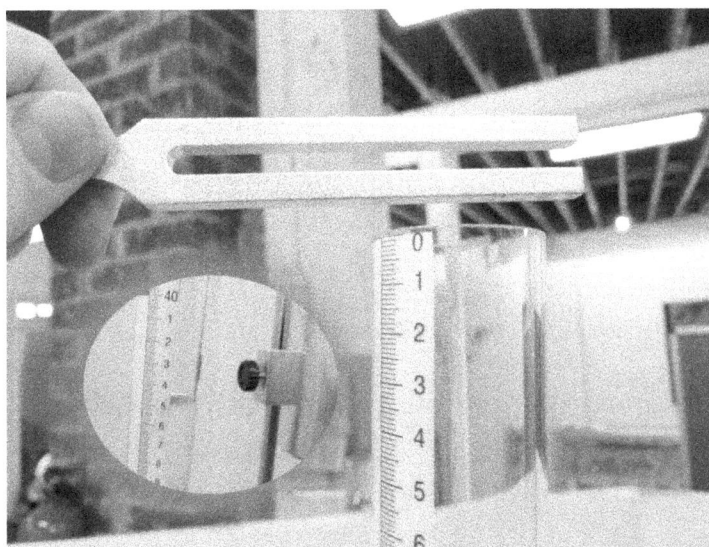

7. Wind Instrument Sounds continued

The quality of the sound emerging from a wind instrument will depend on a number of factors. Obviously, it depends on the length of the resonance tube. But the musical sounds contain not just the fundamental note, but also a number of harmonics. It is the mixture of fundamentals with various proportions of their harmonics which give each instrument its characteristic sounds. The exact mix of these wave forms will be determined by the way in which the air vibration is created, and by the material from which the resonance tube is made.

Flutes

A flute is a fairly simple instrument. It can be considered as a resonance tube, which is closed at both ends. One end really is closed, while the other end is effectively closed by there being a hole in the tube. In fact there are a number of these holes, which can be opened or closed by the fingers. Open holes affect the waves in the enclosed air, and result in longer or shorter columns of vibrating air. As with the air columns in the previous example, there are also harmonic vibrations, and the overall wave form produced by a flute is a composite of these.

The flutist (or flautist, depending on your preference) puts his lower lip adjacent to the embouchure hole. Blowing air over this causes the air inside the flute to vibrate.

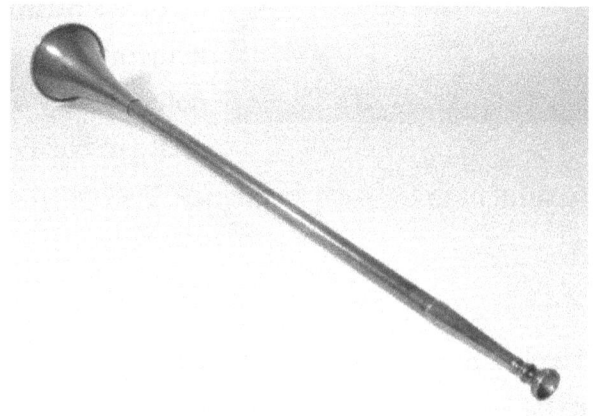

Trumpets and Horns

In the case of a trumpet, the air vibration has to be caused directly at one end of the tube, by vibration of the player's lips and tongue. The long trumpets used by military players in Britain, for ceremonial events, are just long tubes of brass, with the trumpet bell at one end, but no valves. The natural, fundamental note of such an instrument is a B♭, but for convenience it is written as a c. Therefore, every note of music written for the trumpet must be written in a key a tone higher than the sound required.

In the case of the normal trumpets that you will see today, two refinements are added. The first is that the long tube is wrapped around on itself, to shorten the overall length of the instrument. And valves can divert air to longer or shorter pathways, therefore making extra notes possible. Even so, the player must adjust her embouchure in order to play harmonic notes of the fundamental, to get higher pitch sounds.

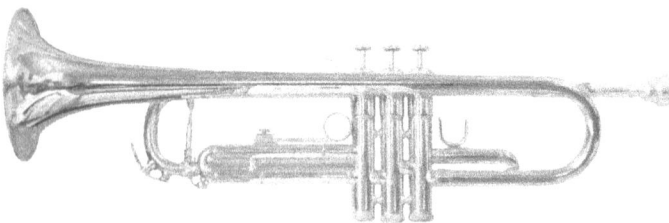

Other brass instruments work in similar ways. The trombone is a very challenging one to play, but is easier to understand scientifically, as

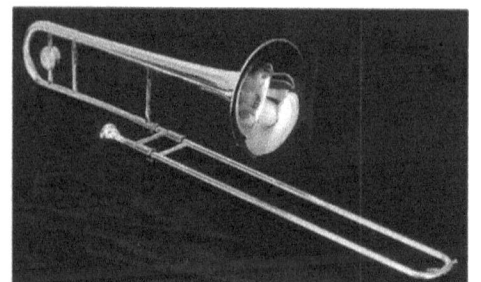

we see the tube being physically lengthened and shortened by the slider.

Reeded Instruments

A number of wind instruments produce sounds by the vibration of reeds. Some have a single reed - these include the clarinet and saxophone families of instruments. Some, such as the oboe family, have a double reed. With all these instruments, the effective length of the vibrating column is altered by holes and keys, in a similar manner to a flute.

Superposition

If two or more waves arrive together, the resultant displacement is equal to the sum of the displacements of each wave. We particularly notice this if the waves are of the same frequency, and at constant phase relationship. In this case, they are said to be coherent. Of course, the waves could be in opposite phase, and then there would be destructive superposition, while if they are in the same phase we will have constructive superposition. The various harmonics produced will superpose, and this is what produces the more complex wave shapes that you may have obtained with the oscilloscope app mentioned earlier. There are devices or applications called spectrum analyzers, which are able to split the complex waves formed by many instruments into their component waves. This analysis of the frequencies made by the natural B♭ sound of the trumpet shows that some harmonics are emphasized more than others, and one

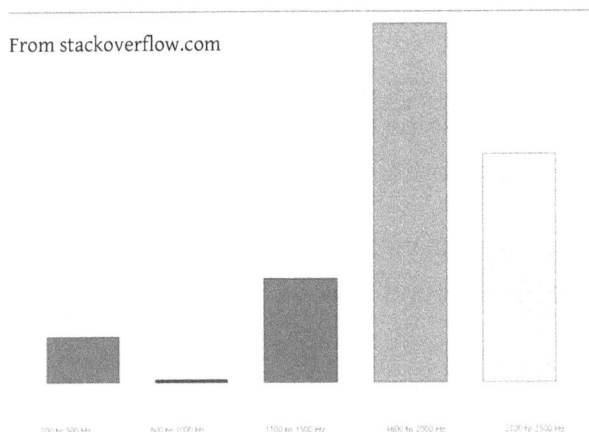

From stackoverflow.com

is virtually missing. Different instruments produce different spectrum analyses, and this explains their different qualities of sound.

For Further Study

1. What is the distance on a standing wave between two adjacent nodes? (Express your answer in terms of the wavelength)

2. Find out what is meant by the term *resonant frequencies*. Clue: the resonance tube experiment relied entirely on this phenomenon.

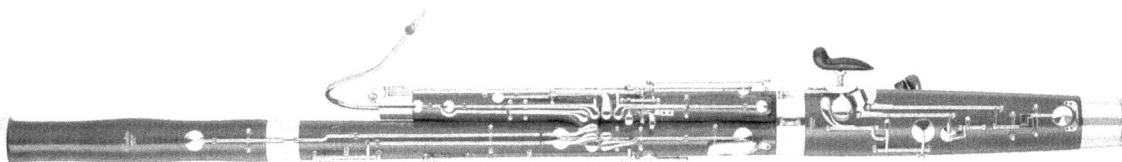

8. Catching Sounds

The movement of sound waves through the air is a physical process. We have already discussed how the waves move by a succession of compressions and rarefactions. This can be seen by a simple experiment where a candle is placed close to a loudspeaker. The candle flame can be seen to move with the physical effects of the sound waves.

The Ear

The most obvious example of a device to collect sound waves is also one of the most sophisticated, yet brilliant in its simplicity. It is the ear. Mammalian ears are all constructed in a similar manner, though the external portion, designed to direct the sound inwards into the middle ear, often differs in shape. We will, however, concentrate just on the structure of the human ear.

The Bible has a lot to say about the ear. In most cases, the word ear is used, not just to describe the actual auditory organ, but also to describe the state of actually hearing. "Incline your ear, O Lord" is a common prayer, asking God not only to hear, but to act. And the same active metaphor is used of our obedience to God's word, rather than just collecting the sounds.

The book of Proverbs reminds us that it is God who was responsible for giving us organs of seeing and hearing. "The hearing ear and the seeing eye, the LORD has made them both", we read in Proberbs 20:12.

The ear can be considered in three parts - outer, middle, and inner. And, of course, we have two of them, so that we can hear in stereo, and get a 3D location on the source of the sound that we hear.

Outer Ear

The outer ear includes the *pinna*, which is the bit we can see, and which is commonly called the ear. The shape of this design is no accident. God has designed it in such a way that it focuses sound waves into the *ear canal* - the hole in the ear. These sound waves will then strike the *tympanic membrane* - or "ear drum", so that it vibrates with the collected sound waves. If that was not clever enough, the next section is a masterpiece of design.

Middle Ear

The ear drum separates the outer ear from the middle ear. In the middle ear, there are three tiny bones - the tiniest bones in the human body. These are the *malleus, incus,* and *stapes.* Those are the official names of the bones, collectively known as *ossicles*, but they are better known by their popular names, based on their shapes, of hammer, anvil, and stirrup. These bones are set vibrating by the ear

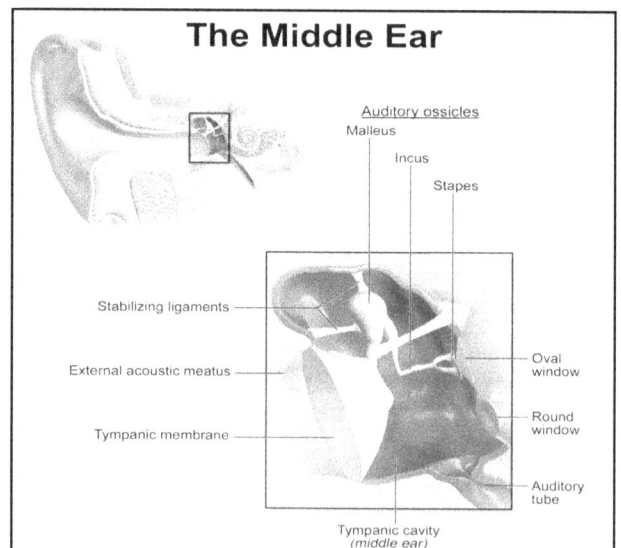

The Middle Ear

Auditory ossicles
Malleus
Incus
Stapes
Stabilizing ligaments
External acoustic meatus
Tympanic membrane
Oval window
Round window
Auditory tube
Tympanic cavity (middle ear)

Blausen.com staff (2014). "Medical gallery of Blausen Medical 2014". WikiJournal of Medicine 1 (2). DOI:10.15347/wjm/2014.010. ISSN 2002-4436, license CC BY-SA 3.0 Unported

drum, and the bones amplify these vibrations. At the same time, certain extraneous frequencies are removed, making a clearer sound. The innermost of the three bones - the stirrup - sets the oval window vibrating, having amplified the sound some 15 - 20 times.

Inner ear

The oval window and round window are both at the edge of an area filled with fluid, which proceeds into the *cochlea* - a spiral organ, which converts the wave pulses into signals, which can be transmitted via the auditory nerve to the brain. The inner ear also contains the semi-circular canals, which help to maintain and monitor balance.

This account of the working of the ear is much abbreviated, but even this can serve to show how well designed by God the ear actually is. The inter-connectedness of all parts of the ear serves to show the impossibility of an organ system like the ear having evolved by random, stepwise chance.

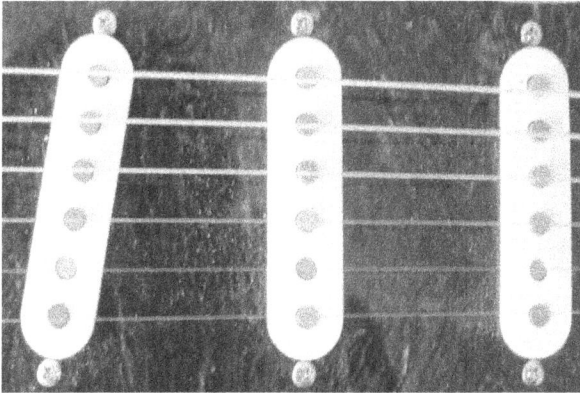

Guitar pickups are basically small piezoelectric microphones.

Microphone

There are many different types of microphone. However, they all have the same purpose - that of turning sound waves into equivalent electrical signals, that can be taken to an amplifier, and / or recording device. As there are so many different types, it would not be productive to list them all here, but we will mention just two.

Carbon Microphone

This is one of the oldest and simplest types. It relies on the fact that one allotrope of carbon - graphite - is an electrical conductor. Ground graphite is loosely packed into a container, and electrical contacts made on either side. If the graphite is fairly loose, then not all graphite particles will be in contact. An electric current is passed through the graphite. If the graphite powder is compressed, then more particles will be touching, causing the effective resistance of the powder to decrease. So, if sound waves are introduced to the graphite reservoir, then electrical signals of higher or lower current will be made by the sound going in. This is a fairly imperfect setup, but used to be used a lot in old-fashioned dial-style telephones.

Piezoelectric Microphone

Some materials produce a voltage when compressed. Potassium sodium tartrate is one such salt crystal. Electrodes attached to the piezoelectric crystal can pick up the variations in voltage created by the sound waves hitting the crystal.

For Further Study

Write a short account, with diagram, of another type of microphone.

9. Recording Sound - The Past

When I first started teaching physics, in the 1980s, it was easy to teach about recorded music, because the main recording media used at that time - which would be vinyl records - were very easy to understand. Today, however, recorded media are much more difficult to understand - though they obviously work better! Recorded media really fall into two categories - analog and digital. Analog media include vinyl records and magnetic tape (cassettes). Digital media include CDs and related items, as well as digital files, such as .wav, .mp3, and .flac. Although the digital media can be difficult to understand, they become easier if you first understand analog recording, so I intend to address that first, even though it is outside the experience of most of you. Fortunately, there has, in the last ten years, been a revival of interest in vinyl records, not as a mass media, but as a niche market, so they are less unknown today than they were at the turn of the millennium!

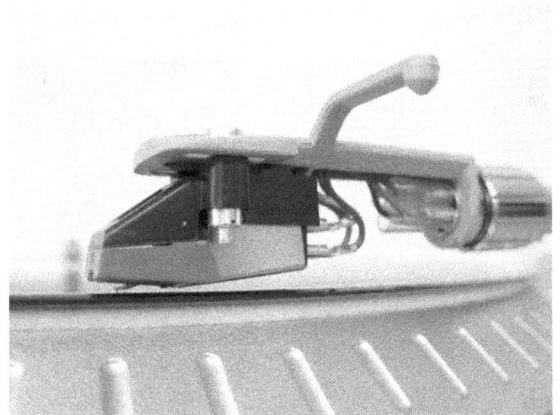

Michelle Hawkins-Thiel, CC BY-SA 2.0 Generic

Your ear is basically an analog device for capturing sounds. We have discussed how the ossicles amplify the sound waves, in order to process them, to send the signals to your brain. There is, therefore, a direct relationship between the wave forms input to the ear, and the wave forms output to the cochlea. We find the same simple relationship with a vinyl record.

When I was a teenager, I had a setup like this.

Vinyl Records

A vinyl record holds its sound (usually music) on a vinyl, plastic disc. This vinyl was usually colored black, simply because early records were made of shellac, which was always black. However, vinyl is clear, and could be made any color, so colored vinyls, while less common, were often made, especially for particular marketing purposes. In the picture of the record player, you can see that the sound is played back, by means of a needle pickup. The needle was usually made from an industrial grade diamond. This needle sat in a groove on the record. An old quiz "catch"-question from the 1970s would be "how many grooves are there on a record?" People tended to guess numbers in the hundreds. But the correct answer was 2. The record has one long groove, spiraling into the center, which the needle followed. But I said the correct answer was 2. That is because both sides of the record were playable, so there was a spiral groove on each side.

If you could look at the groove with a strong magnifying glass, you would see that the inside of the groove was not smooth. It actually contained bumps - peaks and troughs. These simply directly corresponded to the shape of the sound waves. In early records, the sides of the groove were parallel, so one single (monophonic) sound track was produced. This was later refined to stereophonic, with two sound tracks. A double needle sat in the groove, and the two sides of the groove had different bumps and grooves to produce two sound tracks - one for the left hand speaker and one for the right.

Although this system is easy to understand, very few people had the equipment to record their own records. For that possibility, most of us used cassette tapes.

Magnetic Tape

Magnetic tape could also be used to record and play back analog sound. Plastic tapes were coated with metal oxides, which had a limited amount of movement on the tape. These metal oxide particles were all

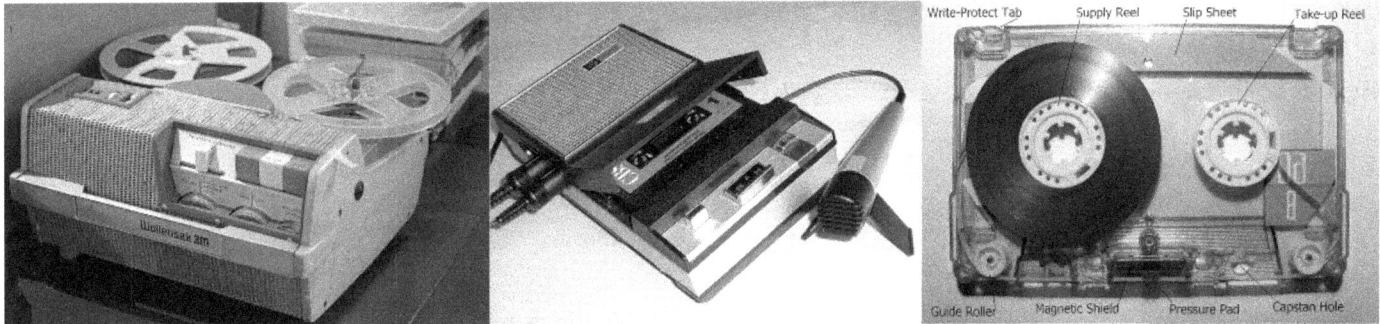

little magnets. Imagine if they all started vertical. Input sound waves could move the magnets, by rotating them away from the vertical. The amount of rotation was directly proportional to the displacement caused by the sound waves recorded on to the tape. Unlike records, systems for recording on to tape were very easy to set up. This convenience became even greater in the mid 1970s, as compact cassettes of tape started to be used, in place of the larger reel-to-reel recorders and players earlier. Cassette technology lasted a very long time. Even today, many car audio systems still have cassette players. The photographs - all from Wikipedia - show a reel-to-reel recorder, a 1970s cassette recorder / player, and one of the portable players from the 1980s, that usually worked with little headphones on a long cord. Most recording studios, up until the advent of digital music, would record music using magnetic tape. After the various recorded tracks were mixed, the signals would be sent to a machine to etch the music on to a metal disc, which was basically the reverse of one side of the vinyl record. Two of these discs would be used to press the record out of semi-molten vinyl.

Problems

Every stage of recording and playing back analog music can lead to amplification of *noise* - by which we mean a sort of sound pollution. Additionally, records could be scratched or broken. Tape could be mangled and ripped. Music on both these media could often be very temporary. Digital sound gave us the ability almost to eliminate noise, and certainly to obtain better methods of storing the music.

10. Recording Sound - The Digital Revolution

Digital technologies are closely allied to computer technologies. It is not part of this course to explain how computer technologies work. That is better left for our unit on communication science, entitled *Get the Message*. The word *digital* in this context refers to numbers. Those numbers are expressed in binary, so that the only digits are 1s and 0s. The stark difference between a 1 and a 0 can easily be expressed in all sorts of ways - by high and low voltages in electronic systems, by wide and negligible rotations of magnetic media, by light being on or off in fibre optics, and by tiny mirrors on a surface being active or inactive, such as on optical recording media - e.g. CDs.

Digitizing a Sound Wave

Here is a simple sinusoidal sound wave.

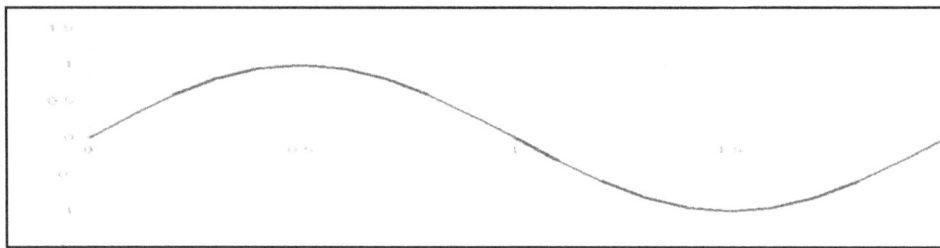

Now imagine that the displacement is measured at rapid, regular intervals, as represented by the vertical lines.

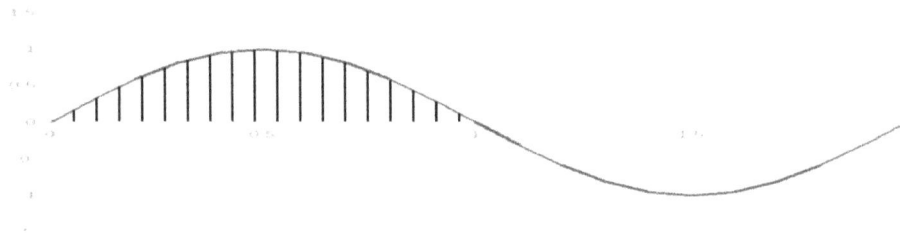

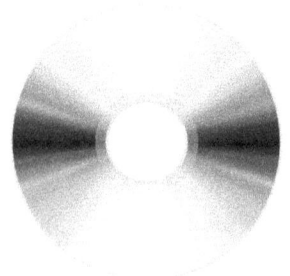

The vertical lines now represent numbers, which can be expressed in binary. It is these numbers (as 1s and 0s) that are transmitted or recorded. To reconstruct the sound from the numbers, we can see from the lines representing the numbers that they seem to describe the sound wave. The shorter the timescale between these number measurements, the more accurately the sound is represented.

Compact Discs (CDs)

The earliest commonly available form of digital recording was the CD. In CD media, the sound has been sampled at 44.1kHz - that is 44,100 times per second. The underside of a CD looks like a mirror - and so it is. In fact, it is a lot of very tiny mirrors. Some of these are set apart at different levels. The mirrored surface is of aluminum, placed on a polycarbonate plastic surface, and protected by a clear protective covering. The CD typically sits mirror side down. A laser is fired upwards at the CD, through a 45° one-way mirror. It hits the mirrored surface, and bounces back to the 45° mirror. Then,

depending on whether it had hit a pit or a bump on the mirror, it will either be reflected at 90° or not, because the pits and bumps are less than a wavelength apart. Thus the collector will receive 1s or 0s, because reflected waves present either constructive or destructive superposition. These represent the digital binary numbers, used to build up the sound wave, as shown above.

In the early days (1980s) CDs were designed just for music. However, they could hold any form of digital information, so began to be used for computer software storage. This led to recordable and rewritable CDs being developed. DVD and BluRay technologies are pretty similar, with much smaller bumps and pit mirrors, in order to hold more information in a disc of the same size.

Early DVD players often included cassette players with them. One photo here shows a 1980s "boombox".

Digital Sound Files

As computer technology developed, it became possible to store digital files of music. These could then be played back, either on computers, or on specialist players (such as mp3 players), which are, in any case, actually small computers. These sound files can have a variety of formats, such as **Waveform Audio File Format** (or WAVE or .wav) on Microsoft systems, or **Audio Interchange File Format** (AIFF) found on Apple systems. Both these formats are of raw, uncompressed audio. The file formats tend to be large, and therefore some formats were developed, whereby algorithms were able to compress information, omitting some of it, where it could be assumed or repeated. The most famous of these compressed formats is **MPEG-1 Audio Layer**, better known as **.mp3**. The compression is a lossy compression - that is information is lost. So a compressed mp3 file cannot later be returned to its uncompressed form. However, mp3s became well known for being small enough easily to download on the slower internet connections we had in the early years of the century.

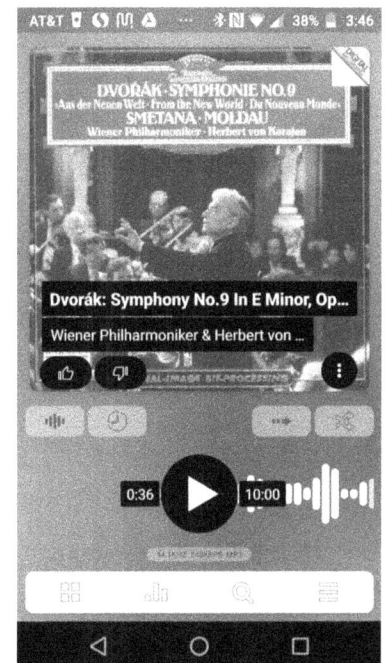

The **Free Lossless Audio Codec** (or FLAC) is a more recent lossless compression. FLAC files will typically be bigger than mp3 files, but there is no loss of information. Most FLAC files offer sound reproduction equal to that on a CD, and some boast of even higher quality to near studio recording standards. MP3s and FLACs are not the only digital sound files in use, but they are probably the most common, and the multiplicity of software music apps on smartphones and tablets has made such musical reproduction widespread. As a lover of classical and other art music, I personally love FLACs, as they give me a near orchestral experience.

PowerAmp *app, playing a FLAC of Dvořák's New World Symphony, on a Lenova smartphone, running Android.*

For Further Study

Research and write notes on other aspects of digital sound not included here.

11. How Stringed Instruments Work

There are many different classes of stringed instruments, but they will all work in a similar way.

Violin Family

Viols were medieval instruments, with a similar appearance to the modern violin family, so the concept of the violin family has been around for centuries. All viols were played upright, like a cello. However, the modern violin is usually placed under the chin, though some traditions place it on the shoulder.

The most well-known members of the violin family are the violin, viola, cello (short for violincello), and double bass. Most family members have four strings, tuned a perfect 5th apart. A perfect 5th note vibrates with a frequency 1.5 times the previous string. Violins are usually tuned to G3-D4-A5-E5, though other tunings are possible. The double bass will usually tune its strings a perfect 4th apart, and will sometimes have a 5th string. The strings are fixed at the bottom end of the instrument, and strung over a bridge. The top end of the strings pass over a small nut, and then are wrapped around tuning pegs.

Photo by Martin Möhler, CC BY-SA 2.0 Germany

There is a finger board under the strings, to enable the vibrations to be shortened or lengthened by the player's left hand. In her right hand, the violinist holds a bow, and this is what is used to cause the strings to vibrate - a feature almost unique to the violin. The sound of the vibrations is amplified, using a soundbox. Actually, there is no real amplification, but the soundbox enables the air inside it to vibrate, and that produces a clearer sound that carries further than just the string itself. Most stringed instruments have a soundbox. The violin's sounds are influenced by the material out of which the strings are made, the material out of which the soundbox is made, the shape of the soundbox, and the characteristic shape of the sound holes (usually f-holes on a violin). In recent years, experiments have been made fitting violin family instruments with piezoelectric microphones under the strings, or abandoning the soundbox altogether and using a magnetic pickup, like an electric guitar.

Guitar Family

And that brings us to the guitar family. Like the violin family, strings vibrate and the sound echoes through a sound box. The strings are attached at the lower end, and, as with a violin, are stretched over a nut at the far end of the fingerboard, and on to tuning keys. However, with guitars, the bridge at the fixed end is much lower than on violins, and is usually a small piece of wood (or metal on electric guitars). The sound hole is usually directly under the strings (though there are variations on this). The tuning keys are usually operated by machine heads. And the finger board has a large number of frets, arranged to play notes at semitone intervals. So the guitarist's fingers are placed behind the point, from which the string is to vibrate, rather than at the exact point, as on a violin.

In the case of most classical guitars, the strings tend to be made of nylon, and the sound box out of wood. Some guitars will be strung with steel strings. However, in the jazz era, there were experiments with metallic soundboxes, and also with f-holes, in place of the normal circular sound hole.

Electric Guitars

Sometimes acoustic guitars are fitted with pickups, comprising of six little piezoelectric microphones, so that a simple electrical signal can be sent to an amplifier. The electric guitar takes this one step further. The soundbox is removed altogether, and magnetic sensors placed underneath the strings, which will be made of steel.

The steel string is therefore vibrating within a magnetic field, and the resultant electrical signal is easy to pick up and send to an amplifier. This system also makes it possible for a number of effect boxes - often operated by the guitarist's foot - to intercept the signal, and make changes to it. There is a huge amount can be written about electric guitars, if this were a music textbook, but the scientific concepts are not too complicated!

Fender Stratocaster - arguably the best known electric guitar. Martin Taylor, CC BY-SA 2.0 Generic

Refining the Sound

Entrepreneur and musician Matt McPherson put his knowledge of music, technology, and physics to use, by redesigning the guitar, in a number of fascinating ways. He noticed several problems with traditional acoustic guitars, upon which he knew he could improve. Matt describes the difference between his guitars and a traditional guitar as like the difference between an upright piano and a grand piano. As a pianist, I understand that comment!

A string which is vibrating is releasing energy. Some of that energy might be wasted, but we want as much as is possible to be converted into high quality sound. If the neck of the guitar is made from inferior material, then it will also vibrate slightly, dissipating energy. So Matt made sure that his guitar necks are much stiffer than normal, to minimize this dissipation.

An example of a McPherson guitar - copyright photo used with permission.

Perhaps, most characteristically, a McPherson guitar has the sound hole in a different place. The sound hole is a low frequency port. A traditional guitar has a sound hole in the most flexible part of the upper diaphragm of the soundbox. This hinders the production of sound. By moving the sound hole, and rethinking the shape of the sound box. Matt has been able to influence the mix of harmonics released by the soundbox, producing the characteristically rich sound.

Other refinements include different types of wood, and even different materials, such as carbon fiber. This is definitely an example of physics meets music, and science meets art.

12. Acoustic Keyboard Instruments

The most significant acoustic keyboard instrument is undoubtedly the piano. But before we discuss the physics of the piano in detail, let's look briefly at two of its antecedents.

Harpsichord

In some ways, almost all acoustic keyboard instruments can be considered a machine methods of playing a harp. The harpsichord contains a large number of strings, of different lengths and thicknesses. The strings are stretched over a bridge and a nut, and each one has its own tuning peg. The keys are really levers, operating a spring-loaded pick or plectrum, which plucks the string on its upward stroke, but brushes harmlessly past on its downward. This plucking action does not allow for a lot of dynamic variability, but the sounds are assisted by a sound board, rather than box, situated beneath the strings.

Clavichord

Closely related to the harpsichord was the clavichord. This does not appear much today, although composers like J.S. Bach wrote a lot of music for

Andreas Ruckers 1646 Harpsichord. CC BY-SA 3.0 Generic.

it, as well as harpsichord. While Bach's harpsichord music is usually played on that instrument, his clavichord music is usually played on the piano these days.

A Steinway Grand Piano

The keyboard levers in the clavichord operated hammers which struck the strings. However, the hammer remained in contact with the string, so the vibrations were soon damped.

Pianoforte

The full name for the piano is the pianoforte - a portmanteau word, combining the Italian words for soft and loud. In my opinion, the piano was a genius of an invention of the classical music era.

As with its antecedents, each piano key is a lever. But the complex mechanism has a number of jobs to do. Each string is damped by a felt hammer. Actually, most notes are comprised of three strings, tuned to the same note - but more on that later. When the key is struck, the damper is removed from the string. At the same time, a hammer strikes the string, but - and this is the genius - immediately bounces away, and held close. Therefore, the string vibrates, undamped. When the key is released, the hammer returns to its seat, and the damper also returns, stopping the string from vibrating. This fascinating mechanism allows for dynamics. The harder a key is played, the harder the string will be struck, and the louder the sound. The strings are pinned, pegged, and bridged in a similar manner to the harpsichord. The piano is usually furnished with two pedals. The right (sustaining) pedal takes all dampers off all strings, while it is depressed, allowing for echo and overlap of sounds. When the pedal is released, all dampers return. The left (muting) pedal moves all hammers slightly left, so that they hit only two, instead of three strings. This quietens the sound. In some pianos, there is insufficient room for hammer movement, so,

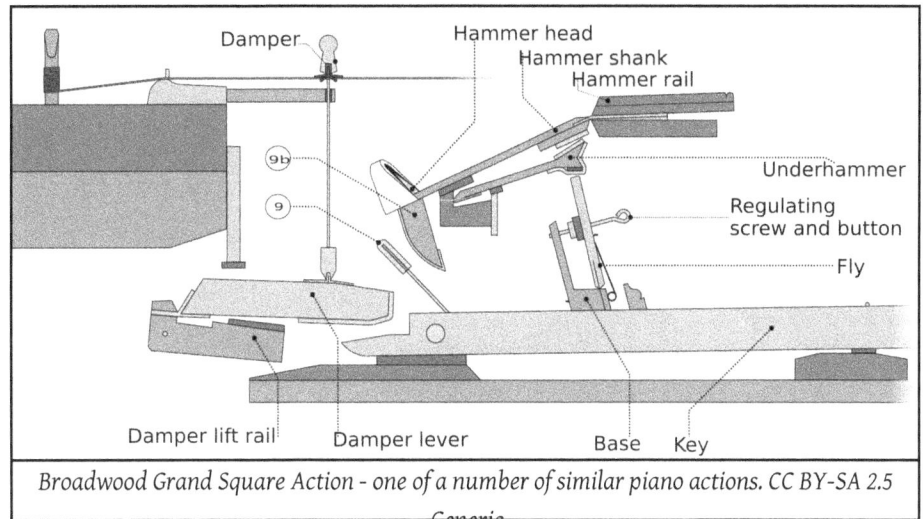

Broadwood Grand Square Action - one of a number of similar piano actions. CC BY-SA 2.5 Canaria

instead, the hammers are moved closer to the strings, making their striking movement shorter, and therefore quieter. The third, middle, pedal found on some pianos is a sostenuto pedal, raising the dampers of keys already pressed, so that selective sustaining can be achieved.

One fascinating aspect of the physics of the piano is the use of three strings for most of the notes (except for lower pitched notes). If an attempt is made to tune all the piano strings perfectly, it is found that, because of the idiosyncrasies of so many strings, it is impossible to do. For example, the piano's seven octaves could be tuned an octave at a time. Then the strings could be tuned a 5th pitch at a time. The same note is reached by both methods, theoretically, but in practice, the coincident note is found to sound very different by the two methods. Therefore, piano strings are tuned by an ingenious compromise, based entirely on physics. Each one of the three strings for one note is tuned separately to the correct pitch. But when the strings of a perfect fifth above are tuned, the tuning is *tempered* - that is, tuned very slightly lower than it "should" be. Many of the harmonics ought to coincide, and as they have been tuned slightly off, there will be interference between the sound waves, causing what is known as *beating*, where the two notes played together go quieter and louder. This effect is very difficult to hear. Over two centuries of piano tuning, it has been calculated how many beats per second should exist between combinations of notes, and the piano tuner will have to measure these. Today there are electronic instruments to help with this, but in the past, tuners had to have exceptionally fine hearing, and an accurate stopwatch. Since the popularity of pianos increased rapidly from 1800 onward, piano tuning became an important profession, as few pianists had the time, skill, or inclination to tune their own instruments. As a bunny trail, this profession was often taken on by blind people, whose loss of one sense often aided their ability in the other. So highly skilled was this process, that the apprenticeship for piano tuners was usually at least five years. The profession is dying out today, with the increased number of electronic pianos. Also, air conditioning and heating, which provides us with comfort, is very detrimental to the condition of pianos, as it tends to dry out the sound board, where the tuning pegs are fixed, preventing strings from holding their pitch.

For Further Study

Find out how 1960s and 70s electric pianos, like the *Fender Rhodes*, work. Write a few descriptive notes.

13. Synthesized Music

How Synthetic Sounds Are Made

A big clue on how synthetic sounds are made can be to re-read the section on digital recording again. This is because synthesized music is like the reverse of that process. Today's synthetic music is really computer generated in form. A digital musical instrument is really a computer, dedicated to producing sounds.

Consider this waveform of a trumpet note.

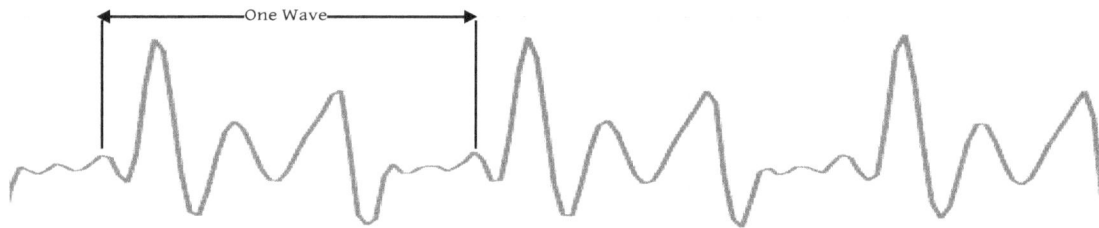

As with recording waves, samples are taken at short intervals - the shorter the interval, the more accurate it will be. These samples are converted into binary numbers. The resulting sample shape is close to that of

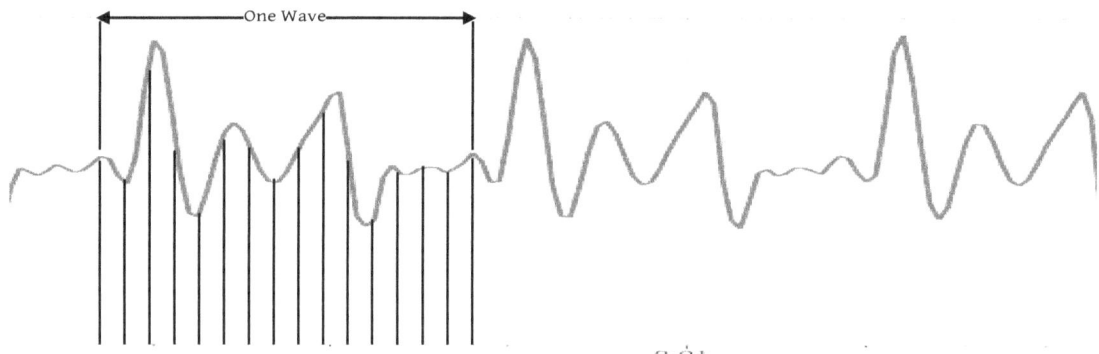

the original trumpet wave. These numbers can be artificially generated by computer, and the resulting sequence of numbers - which simulate the shape of the trumpet sound wave - can be sent to an amplifier. All that is then needed is for a system of producing these waves, at different frequencies, for different

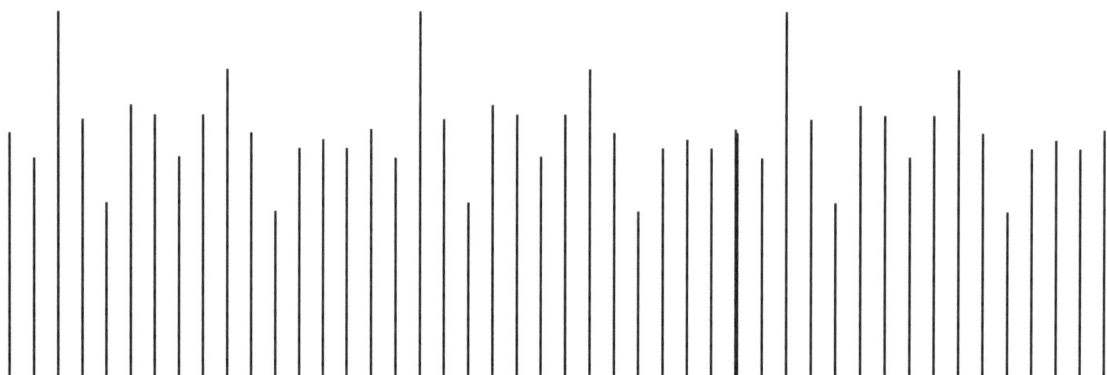

pitches, is produced. The simplest method of doing this is to use a piano style keyboard, where each key is really a switch, to turn on or off the relevant sound. Digital instruments also contain a lot of completely artificial sounds, unrelated to actual musical instruments.

Digital Keyboard Instruments

Lots of sampled waveforms of different instruments can be stored in the drives of these musical computer keyboards. Further refinements would be that the instrument needs to be able to play several notes at once.

Simple keyboard switches are not really sufficient, so weighted keyboards have been developed, that mimic the feel and effect of piano keyboards - that is, the harder they are pressed, the louder the sound will be. Devices called strain gauges can be added to the keyboard mechanism, that will produce electric signals, in proportion to the force used to strike the key.

Onyx Ashanti plays a wind synth. CC BY-SA 2.0 Generic

MIDI

Musical Instrument Digital Interface (MIDI) is a digital protocol, to allow digital musical devices to talk to each other. It is a relatively old technology, having been developed in 1983. However, in January 2019, it was announced that there would be a MIDI 2.0 protocol developed. MIDI enabled the keyboard musical controller to be separate from the musical sample data storage, so that, for example, extra instrument sounds could be added to a keyboard's repertoire.

Non-Keyboard Controllers

Although most synthesized digital music is controlled by a piano-style keyboard, other controls are possible. For example, the **wind controler**, or **wind synth**, is breath controlled, and played like a clarinet or saxophone.

© 2009 JR deSouza of Inspired Instruments Inc., Permission granted on Wikimedia Commons

Afterword

This unit textbook provides an introduction to studies on wave theory, as it pertains to sound waves.

Acknowledgement

I am very grateful to Matt McPherson for his time, in providing extra helpful information for this book.

Further Units

Further physics units will address topics such as *light waves (optics)*, and *electronics*.

Mountain Word Science units currently available (March 2019) are:

Chemistry
Oil
Metals

Chemistry units in production include:
Chemistry on the Farm
Color by Design

Physics units in production include:
Transporters
The Light Fantastic

If you would like support for any of these units, or any other aspects of physics or chemistry for teenagers, then please do not hesitate to contact us at:

highschool@mshcreationcenter.org

Also, we will gradually be adding support materials on the Mountain Word Academy website at:

https://mwacademy.mshcreationcenter.org

All these materials and textbooks take time and resources to produce. Donations to our ministry can be made at our main website:

https://mshcreationcenter.org

Also, see our publications website:

https://justsixdays.com

www.ingramcontent.com/pod-product-compliance
Lightning Source LLC
Chambersburg PA
CBHW080941030426
42339CB00008B/473